AF229727

In loving Memory Of

Buttons
Fluffy
Caesar
September
Mehitabel
Mehitabel 2
Mohamed Ali
Thomas O'Leary
Belle
Emma
Willie Mays
Huckleberry
Rudolph Rutabaga
and others my memory has lost

Dedication

Dedicated to my family who have shared my affection for, and
my life with my wonderful furry friends.

Cosy up,
there's plenty
of room

Better
View

Squeezing
through.

Who wants a
snowy walk?

Hey, that's
my seat.

Fetch

MEOW!
And he
has
never
played
fetch
again.

Who
needs
privacy

ARGH!!

Kitty, kitties. Where are you?

Willie finds a
fountain.

My turn.

Three make a line.

Hucky, NO!

Oh
Hucky,
why didn't
you listen
to me?

September,
you are moving.

NYC is great!

Hamburgers for lunch!

Can't take the street out of a street cat.

What's that?

Let's see.

Purrfect

New horizons

Don't mind me.

Midnight snack

Help!

Goodbye

All are comfy.

9 781917 438469